The Rainbow Bridge
…a dog's story

By Henley Harrison West
Typed by Judith Kristen

ISBN: #978-1-9743321-7-5

This book is printed on acid free paper.

Cover art by: Myra Matias-Taylor
Illustration by: Myra Matias-Taylor
Cover design by: Tim Litostansky
Animal loving Editors one and all: Carol Bauman, Sandra
Lippman, and Andrew Poland
First published by Aquinas & Krone Publishing, LLC
April 10, 2010
Please visit: www.judithkristen.com

Part of the proceeds from this book
will benefit animal rescue.

This book is dedicated to all of the kind, compassionate souls who have given so much of themselves, in so many different ways, to make the world a better place for our animal friends.

Foreword

The concept of The Rainbow Bridge is a beautiful one and although the poem of the same name is written by an 'Unknown Author', it has helped to heal the hearts of many whose loyal and loving furry family members have left their much-adored, and adoring, 'uprights' for a new life over that very bridge.

This lengthier version comes on the heels of the loss of our sheepdog, Henley, and is written in his own voice, as was his book, *My Name is Henley: my life and times as a rescued dog.*

His loss not only affected our immediate family and close friends, but the thousands of children he visited over the years. Less than seventy-two hours after Henley's passing I drove to the two schools Henley visited most often – Good Intent School in Deptford, New Jersey (where he was their mascot), and Carson School in Pennsauken where his story was embraced and even shared with students in Manchester, England, via computer technology called: "Distance Learning."

The children were heartbroken and at odds with themselves as how to deal with the pain of their loss. Henley was more than a dog to the students, he represented so many things to them: a rough beginning in life, abandoned, sickly, hungry, unloved, lacking decent shelter, wanting someone to care, needing someone to be a strong and steady force in his life...and looking for a safe place to land. Sadly, far too many of the urban students Henley visited over the years identified with him and where he came from, and so they embraced Henley, his story, and his mission.

He was one of them. They applauded his rise from neglect and abuse to become a great and most appreciated and honored humane education ambassador.

He was more than words on paper.

More than a character in a book.

He became his audience's friend and an example of the good things that happen when one finds a way to rise above some pretty sad and scary circumstances. The kids grew to realize that if a dog could make a difference in two-legged and four-legged lives...well then, why couldn't they?

And that was the whole point of Henley's mission of rescue and adoption. To teach these children to live a life that values life.

So, I began to put together this story (at the time I only had three chapters finished) and I took the first twelve pages to school and the kids sat on the edge of their seats as they heard Henley's voice, now from another place, and it gave them a sense of closure. It also gave them the understanding that they should celebrate this dog's life and not just mourn his loss. Yes, the tears and sadness are normal, feeling his loss is normal, and so is moving forward – to honor him.

Immediately plans were made to hold a Celebration Day at both schools – not only for Henley but for all of the students' and teachers' animals, and for animals everywhere who had taken that trip across The Rainbow Bridge. Also, this Celebration Day embraces Henley's mission, as children, teachers, family and friends continue to donate much needed items to our furry friends in shelters still awaiting that special someone to love.

May this gentle sheepdog's words also give you comfort, smiles, understanding, and a reason to celebrate rich memories that live on and on.

Even in the darkest of situations, you can find the light…if you look in the right places.

And this book is one of those places.

Judith Kristen
March 19th, 2010

Chapter One

It was a dark and stormy night...

I always wanted to write that at the beginning of a story.

But it actually *was* a dark and stormy night.

Let me explain…

About six weeks ago I really started to feel my age. I was less than two months shy of my twelfth birthday, and my old legs definitely weren't working like they used to. It was getting harder to get up and walk around. And, at times, even a bit painful. Then one morning, I just collapsed. My back legs totally gave out on me. I tried to get up and I struggled a bit but I fell right back down again. I wasn't really scared but it didn't make me too happy either, that's for sure. Straight away, Mom and Dad being the good Mom and Dad that they are, took me to my veterinarian, Dr. Vaughn. He gave me some medicine, I got a shot, and then he ran a few tests. I wasn't exactly 100% when he was done with me but I sure was feeling a whole lot better than when I first got there!

Chapter Two

Every day I had a hard time standing up – but I made it.

I had to! I had plans.

See, I was particularly looking forward to my twelfth birthday because that meant lots of extra sheepdog love and a birthday cupcake from the L&M Bakery! I certainly wasn't about to miss out on that!

Well, the day finally came, and wobbly old me celebrated my twelfth birthday on March 10th, 2010! Me, Mom, Dad, Jonny, sheepdog sisters: Cassie and Abbey, and my five feline friends: Miss Rose, Holly, Mookie, Ned and my Puppy Cat, Cynthia. We all had a wonderful time! We even got to wear party hats! My favorite gifts of all were getting hugs and kisses from Mom and Dad, and of course, my birthday cupcake from the L&M Bakery. It was delicious!

But three days later, came the dark and stormy night I was talking to you about earlier.

I always slept upstairs with Mom and Dad – *always*. But that night I just couldn't make it up the steps, so my parents made me comfortable downstairs. I was with my sheepdog friends and all the kitties, so I had company and I didn't feel alone.

"I like having you sleep downstairs with me, Hen," Cynthia said gently resting her head on my big shaggy paws. *"You're nice and warm."*

"Well, it's nice to be here with you too."

"How are your legs feeling, Henley?"

"Not so good tonight, Cyn."

"How come?"

"I'm just gettin' old. That's all."

Cynthia snuggled into my paw. *"Is this gonna be a circle of life story?"*

"You mean, am I going to die?"

"Well…yeah."

"Cyn…when our time comes, it comes."

"And I shouldn't be scared?"

"Haven't you heard the story about The Rainbow Bridge?"

Cynthia looked up into my eyes. *"I think I heard Mandy talk about it when I was just a kitten. It was sort of a poem, wasn't it?"*

"Sort of. Would you like to hear it?"

"Sure."

"Okay... there's a lot of versions of it but here's how it was told to me. You ready?"

"Yup!"

"Just this side of heaven is a place called The Rainbow Bridge. When an animal dies that has been especially close to someone here on earth, that pet goes to The Rainbow Bridge. There are beautiful meadows, lush fields, and flower-filled hills and valleys for all of our special friends so they can run, jump, and play together. It is magnificent! There's always plenty of food, yummy treats, fresh water, glorious sunshine, and our animal friends are warm, safe, and comfortable. The animals who had been ill and old are restored to health and have the energy and stamina of a six-month old puppy; those who were hurt or disabled are made whole and strong again, too. All of the Bridge's residents are happy and content, except for one thing – they each miss someone who was very special to them, someone who had to be left behind. They all run and play together, but the day comes when one suddenly stops and looks

off into the distance. His bright eyes are intent; his eager body quivers, then, suddenly, he begins to run from the group, flying over the green grass, his legs carrying him faster and faster. He spots the one who had to be left behind. And then they finally meet, and they cling together in a joyous reunion, never to be parted again. The happy kisses rain upon the animal's face; hands again caress that beloved head, as the animal looks once more into the loving eyes of that very special someone, so long gone from your life but never, ever absent from your heart."

"That's a beautiful story, Henley."

"I think so too. My mother told me that when I was just a baby."

"So, someday we'll see each other at The Rainbow Bridge?"

"Someday."

"And will I see Mandy again?"

"Of course you will."

"You're a great dog, you know that? Even with your wobbly old legs."

I smiled at her. "I take that as the highest compliment, Miss Cynthia."

Chapter Three

Later that evening I decided to get up for a little drink of water but my legs weren't cooperating and I couldn't stand up. No one was around at the time because Jonny was asleep, and so were Mom and Dad. I decided to give my legs a break and get some additional shut-eye. I could have barked for some help but I wasn't really all that thirsty. I figured I'd wait for Mom and Dad to walk down the steps early in the morning. I'd get something to drink then.

Why can't I get up? What's wrong with me?!!!

Chapter Four

Early the next morning, as soon as I saw my Dad's smiling face, I wagged my butt and started to get up, but even my front legs didn't work. Dad called for Mom and she ran right down the staircase.

"What's the matter, He-Boy?" Mom said patting my head.

I don't know. This is the craziest thing!

Dad tried to get me up and I was doing my best to help him but I fell right back down again.

Dad! I can't walk!

Mom brought me over a drink of water, and it sure felt good – nice and fresh and cool. Then she walked to the kitchen and brought me back some of my favorite treats. I ate them almost as fast as I ate my birthday cupcake.

Well, at least nothin's wrong with my appetite! But these legs?!

Jonny walked into the living room and then he and Dad tried to help me up. Nothing worked. I couldn't walk anymore. My legs just gave out on me – and I was exhausted.

Dad sat on the floor and talked to me. He touched my legs, but I couldn't feel too much. I saw Mom take the phone from the charger and walk into the kitchen. A few minutes later she called for Dad and then Jonny sat with me for a while. Jon gave me some more water and a bite to eat. It tasted good.

Thanks, Jon Boy.

Mom made a few more phone calls and then Dad said we were going for a ride over to the veterinarian's office.

Great! I always love a good car ride! But how can I get into the car?

The weather wasn't cooperating either. It was overcast, damp, foggy, and still raining – a continuation of the dark and stormy night that had just passed me by.

Dad located Mom's nice soft blanket that she wraps around herself when she watches TV and placed it on the floor next to me. I sniffed it. It smelled wonderful... just like my Mom.

Chapter Five

Dad and Jonny lifted me onto Mom's blanket, Mom opened the door, and soon I was on my way into the car. I saw all five cats sitting in the window. Then I saw two shaggy sheepdog faces staring out at me from the window next to that.

Cassie and Abbey just looked at me, but I saw the love in their eyes and it made me feel happy. Ned, Holly, and Rose sat there and watched me too. Their energy felt nothing less than positive.

Mookie swished his tail and said, *"You're a grand old dog, Henley."*

I smiled.

My Puppy Cat squeaked, *"Are you coming right home, Hen?"*

"I'm not so sure. But if I don't, Cyn..."

"Oh, Henley, don't say that..."

"Come on," I smiled at her, "buck up... you know how it goes."

I could barely hear her as she whispered, "I know. If you don't come back home...then I'll see you at The Rainbow Bridge."

"That's the way it works, Puppy Cat. Don't worry, no matter what happens, you'll be hearing from me again."

"Promise?"

"I promise."

Chapter Six

Dad turned the ignition on to start the car while Mom and I sat in the back seat. She covered me with another blanket and I was nice and comfortable. Jon stayed home with the rest of my furry family. He gave me a big hug and a kiss right before he closed the door.

"I love you, Henley."

I love you too, Jonny Boy!

As we started to pull away from the house Mom lifted me up a bit so I could see all of my family still sitting there with their faces staring at me from the windows.

"So long my friends!" I smiled as Mom cuddled close to me.

"So long, Henley!"

"Bye, Hen!"

"I love you, Henley!"

"You're the best, Hen!"

"Peace and Love to you, Dear Henny Boy!"
"All good things to you, Henley!"
"A safe journey, my friend!"

Then we pulled out of the driveway and there we were riding through the same old streets that I rode every day with Mom. Even though it was still raining a bit, Mom opened the windows in the back so I could get some fresh air, and feel a little of that sweet rain on my face. It felt wonderful.

I looked out of the window and saw some small flowers starting to rise up from the dirt, trees with little buds on them, birds singing beautiful songs, and cute, fuzzy gray squirrels running across the street with tiny twigs in their mouths ready to build a summer home in someone's oak tree.

Yes, the world really is a beautiful place…if you look in the right places.

Chapter Seven

Within fifteen minutes we arrived at the Vet's office and I needed more help getting out of the car. The vet and the nurses used a little blue plastic and mesh stretcher to help get me out of the car. I was still snuggled in Mom's blanket, so I was really quite comfortable even with all of the activity.

I was taken to a room where I had been many times before. There were cute pictures on the wall of other dogs, cats, horses, birds...I always liked that room.

The doctor looked me over and a few of the girls who worked in the office stopped by to tell me they were happy to see me! I thought that was sweet.

Mom and Dad rested beside me as the doctor put a tube into my arm. At my age I was used to needles so I didn't even flinch. I just felt like everything was as it should be. You know, we animals are super sensitive to our surroundings; it's a natural instinct. And I felt wonderful. Except for my old legs that wouldn't work anymore.

Mom and Dad kept petting me, they were talking to me about how much fun we had on our walks in the park (I liked to run there), when I first went swimming (I did pretty good), and how cute I always looked hanging my shaggy head out of the car window.

Well, of course I'm cute!

Mom sang to me, Dad scratched my ears, and then I started to feel a little sleepy. The last thing I remember was Mom saying, "I love you, Hen"…and then I lifted my head and I kissed her right on the face.

And then you know what happened?

…THIS was amazing!!!!

Chapter Eight

"Psssssst, Henley! Over here, Buddy!!!!"

"MANDY?!!!"

"Of course, Mandy! Who were you expecting? Rin-Tin-Tin?!"

"I mean, what are you doin' back here in the doctor's office?"

"Hen...get the hair outta your eyes and look around!"

And so I did.

"WOW! Is this some kind of dream? Hey! Look at me! I'm standing! I'M WALKING!!!!" I started to bounce around like a puppy. "LOOK, MANDY!!! I'M..."

"Hen, this is The Rainbow Bridge. That's why you can..."

"What?!"

"I said, **this** is The Rainbow Bridge and..."

"It is?! So what am I doing here?!"

"Henley..."

"You mean, I???!!!"

"Yes. You've crossed over to the other side. That's why we're together again!"

"But...but you're a cat! You have eight more lives left! What are you still doing here?"

She swished her tail in my face. *"Truth be told, old friend, I* **asked** *to stay here. I wanted to wait for you."*

"You're still the sweetheart I remember, Miss Manners! How very, very thoughtful of you."

She nodded. *"Well, I have my moments."*

"But...but Mom and Dad? And Miss Rose and my Puppy Cat and..."

"Hen, it's just like when I passed. It's the circle of life. They know. They understand."

"Geez, I had no idea that I would...I mean, Mom and Dad were petting me and singing to me and..."

"And what, Hen?"

"Well, I didn't pick up on any sad feelings, nothing negative at all, so I didn't expect to...well, you know..."

Mandy continued, *"Henley, Mom and Dad learned a few things over the years. They watched us. They understood that you pick up on those feelings — their joy, sadness, worry, fear, happiness...so they gave you the joy and happiness and not the fear and worry. They wanted love and goodness to be the last things you felt while you were still on earth."*

"They're such thoughtful humans, Mandy."

"Yes they are, Hen. In fact, most humans are when they learn to open their hearts to the bigger picture of life. Learning to live a life that values life is what it's all about."

I gave my feline friend a loving nudge and smiled at her.

"So," she said smiling back into my eyes, *"now that you're here, are you ready for the royal Rainbow Bridge Tour?"*

"SURE!"

"Then, let's go! Henley old boy, this is a study in Happiness 101!"

And when Mandy said, *"Let's go!"* you shoulda seen me. I was running around like a six-month-old puppy!

"Hey! Slow down, Hen!" She laughed. *"Take time to smell the roses!"*

Chapter Nine

Roses?!

When Mandy said roses, she meant it! There we were in a huge valley filled with beautiful roses of every size and magnificent color imaginable! There had to be a million of them! A soft breeze blew and some petals fell onto my nose. They smelled absolutely delightful.

Then I rolled around on my back and wiggled all of my legs into the air like I used to when I was a pup. *"Woo-Hoo! Man, this feels good!"*

"Come on, Hen...over here!" Mandy called to me. *"Over here!"*

WOW! More amazing things: horses galloping around in the most beautiful meadow you will ever see, kitties scampering up trees and around large flowering shrubs, dogs running and playing together, jumping over each other, diving into crystal clear water and swimming directly under a soft waterfall. Then we watched as they climbed on top of huge sparkling rocks to shake themselves dry and rest in the warmth of the sun. Speaking of the sun, overhead was a sky very, very different from the one I remembered on earth. It was the bluest blue I had ever seen, and there were rainbows! Not just one rainbow, but seven!

"*Seven rainbows!*" I said. "*That is incredible!*"

"*Oh, it's not always seven, Henley. Sometimes it's a few less or lots more. They like to change it up to keep things interesting! Many times I've even seen a hundred of them!*"

"*A hundred rainbows?! All at once?!*"

"*Yup! That happens when one of us has that special someone cross over the bridge to be with us again.*"

"*Wow! That must really be something! I can't wait to see that!*"

"*You'll see it, Henley. It happens plenty of times.*"

"*And then someday…well, then someday…*"

"Yes Hen, someday those hundred rainbows will be for us, and we'll see Mom or Dad again. Or maybe they'll even come in together. Ya never know."

"Mandy?"

"What is it, Sheepdog?"

"So...what happens to all the animals who never knew love and kindness? You know, who never had people to love them like we did?"

She smiled at me. "Henley, every animal that ever was comes here and they all find happiness, love, and kindness. That's what The Rainbow Bridge is all about."

I took all of her words in very carefully and then made myself comfortable on the softest grass I ever felt beneath me. I looked straight at Mandy. "Miss Manners?"

"Yes, Hen?"

"I really missed you. I mean, I understood the circle of life as all animals do, but..."

"I know. I missed you too Henley, but...it's not a real sad kind of missing, is it?"

"No. It wasn't sad. It was a wonderful feeling of remembering what we had, an acceptance of the natural course of events, and the knowledge that we really would see each other again someday."

"Good dog!" She smiled at me.

"So, my dear Miss Manners…what did you miss most about me?"

"Well…I think it was when you tried to chase your tail."

"But Mandy, I don't have a tail."

"I know," she smiled, "that's what made it so funny."

Chapter Ten

As we walked along, scampered along, strolled along, and ran around this beautiful never-ending countryside, I had to make a comment.

"This is more than I ever expected! Wow! I bet Dad and Jonny wish they had a TV set that could make things look like all this!"

"Oh, earthly technology," Mandy chuckled. *"Well, this is HD up here too, Henley."*

"It is?"

"Yup…_H_eaven's _D_elight!"

Chapter Eleven

"Yo, Hen!"

"What?"

"I've got another surprise for you! A BIG surprise!" Mandy said as she scampered toward another charming, picturesque hill.

"What is it?!"

"Just come on! Get over here!"

As we stood atop a very high hill I saw lots of dogs running toward us. I heard them call to me, *"HENLEY! HEY, HENLEY!!!"*

As they drew closer I noticed who they were. They were my family! My pack! My sheepdog Mom and Dad, my sisters and brothers, and lots of other dogs that I knew in my life: Sparky from the rescue shelter in Hoboken...my friend, Jackie Dunion's dog, Bridget, Grannie Annie's boy, Charlie, Mindy's Shylow, friend Patty Mehaffey's dog, Teddy, and old pals: Lenny, Angus, Jedi, who were my buddies from the dog park in Philadelphia. Then there was my Dad's German Shepherd that he had when he was a little boy – Sandy, Mom's old dogs: Suzie, Buttons, Chris, Cyndy, Ralph, Martha, Fred, Charlie, Winston, Harry, Rocky and Addison, and, much to my surprise, there was also that scared, hungry, and dirty little pooch that Mom and I saw on Rodman street when I was just a youngster. But he sure looked handsome and well-cared for now! What a great bunch of dogs!!!

All of them surrounded me and we played and rolled around in the soft, emerald-green grass. We traded stories of our lives on earth and marveled at the beauty and happiness here at The Rainbow Bridge. It was fabulous! And, out of nowhere appeared sparkling silver bowls of dog food and water and there were even seven large nearby bushes that had the yummiest of treats hanging all over them! What a party!

I was so happy to see my Sheepdog Mom and Dad and they were very happy to see me. They said they kept an eye on me after they got to The Rainbow Bridge. They were delighted I had a very happy home and that I made my mark as a rescued dog, a puppy mill survivor, and that I did my best to help people (especially children) know that the best animal in the world is one that you adopt and give a second chance at life …maybe even a third or fourth chance.

My old pal from Rodman Street couldn't agree more.

"Henley," he said to me, *"when you called to me as I was running across the street, I wanted to turn around and stay with you, but I was so scared. I just ran away from a home where they beat me and didn't feed me, and they wanted me to fight other dogs."*

"Fight other dogs?!"

"It was horrible. I LOVE dogs! We're all brothers and sisters. I didn't wanna fight."

"You poor thing."

"Then they would dump me in the basement, or I was left outside in the heat or the cold, the snow or the rain. When I first saw you I trusted you because you looked happy and well-fed and well-cared for, but I was in panic-mode and so I just kept running."

I placed my paw over his. *"How awful that some human beings would be so cruel to a dear, sweet dog like you. What happened after that?"*

"Well, then I found an alley way and I hid there for a while to catch my breath and then I decided I'd go out to look for you and your Mom."

"You did?"

"I did. But I couldn't find you. Yet, as luck would have it, another dog and his Mom came by and saw me. He had a nice Mom too and she talked to me in a sweet voice and...and so I followed them home."

"And then?"

"And then I got my second chance at life. I even got a name for the very first time ever!"

"How wonderful! What did she call you?"

"Prince."

"Wow! That's a great name!"

"Well, my Mom said it was time I was treated like one, so she gave me a name that fit."

"I'm happy for you, Prince."

"And I'm grateful to you, Hen. I don't think I would have found room in my heart for her and her dog Ollie, if I didn't give that precious second thought to the kindness you displayed to me. I gave them a chance because of you...and then they gave **me** one."

"I love happily ever afters, don't you, Prince?"

"I sure do, Henley...I sure do!"

Prince and I, my Sheepdog Mom and Dad, and all the rest of the gang played around for a while longer, we ate some more food and treats, drank some of that deliciously clear, fresh water and then...they had to leave.

"So soon?" I asked.

"We'll be back, Henley," my Sheepdog Mom announced, *"we're just your welcoming committee, you know, like Mandy is your tour guide."*

"Oh...I get it! Well, goodbye!!! See you all later!!! Thanks for the warm welcome! It was wonderful to see you!!! I had LOTS of fun!!!"

Mandy and I once again stood at the top of the hill and watched all of them jump, run, dart, dash, and scamper all the way down into the valley and then into the beautiful mist by what looked like another piece of huge farmland.

"What's down there?" I asked Mandy.

"Oh, lotsa things. Wanna see?"

"Sure!"

Chapter Twelve

We started to walk down the hill and Mandy explained where we were going.

"First, to the right of the winding, honeysuckle vines is a wonderful area where you can rest or nap in what they call 'early morning light,' and then, next to that is another soft, grassy hill where you can rest in what they call 'early evening light.'"

"No kidding?!"

"Yup. No kidding!"

"Then there's a place called Starland. I love that place!"

"What is it?"

"It's a beautiful lake surrounded by pine trees and flowers and trailing vines, berry trees, fruit trees...and it's always nighttime there. And the sky has at least a trillion-gazillion stars in it, and there's comets and meteors too! The twinkling never ends. It's totally entertaining and totally relaxing. You'll love it!"

"I bet I will! And what else?"

"Well, there's this big area with a magical tree named Fern right in the middle of the field and…"

"And?"

"You just walk up to Miss Fern and ask to enjoy a particular season or weather condition."

"Noooooooooo."

"Yessssssss!!!" She smiled at me. "If you want a sparkling, alpine snowfall, just ask. A beautiful, crisp, autumn day? Just ask. Summertime by the ocean? Just ask. The first flowers of Spring? Some rain? Wind?"

"I get it…just ask!"

"Yup! It's **just** that easy!"

"Wow! I can hardly imagine what could be next!"

Mandy smiled at me. "Let me take you for another little walk. I think you'll like this one best of all — you being a sheepdog and all that."

"What is it?"

"Come on. Follow me. You'll see soon enough."

Mandy and I walked past the honeysuckle vines, into the early morning light, the early evening light, and then toward Starland.

Along the way Mandy introduced me to Fern, The Magical Tree! I liked her a lot!

"Hey, Henley," Fern smiled, "Stop by and see me later. I've got a special springtime that's got your name written all over it."

I smiled back, "You can count on it!"

We both waved goodbye to Miss Fern and before I knew it, we arrived at the place Mandy thought I would really enjoy! And, oh boy...did I!

"WOW! A dozen full moons?!"

"Yup! How cool is that?! You can have your pick and howl at as many as you like any time at all."

"This really is heaven isn't it?"

Mandy smiled at me. *"Now let me show you one more thing..."*

We walked up a soft, comfortable dirt road that was surrounded by tall weeping willows, mighty oak trees and quite a few very sturdy and sincere-looking maple trees.

As we reached our destination I saw one very long row of what looked to me like oversized computer monitors.

"What are these doing here?" I asked Miss Manners.

"This is a special place where you can go and see what's happening back on earth. You know, a look at Mom and Dad, Jonny, the kitties, Cassie and Abbey, the kids at school..."

"Really?! How cool is that?!"

"Yes! Your full name will flash on the screen, you run over to it, push your paw up against the monitor and then just ask for what you want to see!"

As soon as Mandy said that to me I ran as fast as I could in the direction of heavenly technology.

I ran along each unoccupied screen looking for my name to light up. When I came to the end of the very long row, one of the other dogs talked to me.

"Henley?"

"Yes."

"My name is Elwood, I was your Mom's friend Shelly's dog."

"OH! Elwood! I remember my mother talking about you! How is your Mom doing?"

"I was just checking in. She was taking Romie, the new pup, out for a walk." Elwood laughed. *"Romie has a lot to learn, but, she's only a baby. My Mom has enough love and patience to help her, so...she'll be fine!"*

"Hey! Can I see my Mom on your screen?"

"No, Hen."

"Why not?!"

"Well…"

By then Mandy was right beside me and she answered for Elwood. "Because Henley…you're new here and there's a three-month waiting period until you can use the monitor."

"Why?"

"Our human families need a little time to adjust to our loss. So, we give it three months until we can see them again."

I shook my shaggy head.

"Hen…you wouldn't want to see Mom and Dad unhappy or crying or…"

"Unhappy? Crying? But they were wonderful to me, remember? They sang to me, they pet me, there wasn't a tear, they learned our ways!"

"Well Henley, that's partially true. But after you were gone, some tears fell…their hearts ached. They were strong for you, but remember Hen…they're only human."

"But…"

"The 'uprights' run on this thing called reason, and sometimes it's not very reasonable. We animals run on instinct, universal laws, and we accept the circle of life not just on certain occasions, but 100% of the time."

"So Mom and Dad failed?"

"No Henley…they did right by you, they just need to learn to do that kind of thing more often. Again, they're only human. But, maybe by watching the ease and honesty and acceptance in which all animals live they'll learn to understand how to make it work a little better in their own lives."

"I see. Okay…so I have three months to wait and well…what will we do in the meantime?"

"Hen! We're just gonna have lots and lots of fun! Come on!!!"

I felt tremendous happiness as I watched Mandy scamper down the hill – back to Starland.

"HEY, MISS MANNERS!!!! WAIT FOR ME!!!!!"

Chapter Thirteen

One day (I guess you could call it 'a day') I was resting by one of those huge sparkly rocks after going for a swim when Mandy patted me on the shoulder.

"Hen! You gotta wake up! Look what's happening!"

I shook my head and opened my eyes really wide. I heard all kinds of animals laughing and barking and meowing, and I heard music, and beautiful singing, too. Then I watched as Mandy's paw pointed into the air. I sat straight up and watched as the bluest blue sky I ever saw filled with exactly one hundred rainbows!

"It's one of our friends' Special Someone Day! Come on, Hen! Let's see who it is!"

"You mean?"

"YES! Today's the day when one of our friends is reunited with someone they left

behind…*someone they dearly loved and someone who dearly loved them! It's time! Come on!!!*"

I danced around like a puppy. It was just so exciting!

"Let's see who it is!!"

Mandy and I scampered toward The Rainbow Bridge. Everyone was buzzing about who would be walking over the bridge and whose name would be called to step forward to meet their special someone.

Suddenly the rainbows started to sparkle, roses grew on the bridge trestle, and a choir of Angel fish sang the sweetest music my ears had ever heard, then, in the midst of all of that beauty and wonder, a voice spoke to us and we all became silent.

"The Rainbow Bridge once again celebrates love, friendship, peace, compassion, faith, and loyalty. Today we ask our very own Prince

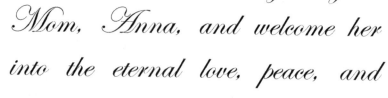

McMillan of Philadelphia to please come forward to greet your Mom, Anna, and welcome her into the eternal love, peace, and happiness she so rightfully deserves."

Suddenly, there was joy, pure joy, coming from voices everywhere.

"It's Prince!!!"

"Prince from Philadelphia!"

"Today is Prince's Day!"

I turned toward Mandy. *"It's our Prince, Mandy! The dog I saw on Rodman Street all those years ago when I was out for a walk with Mom!"*

"Indeed it is," she smiled.

Then, out of the blue (literally), a magnificent white light appeared at the far end of the bridge. And at that very same moment, rose petals fell onto the bridge's walkway and, running happily toward the light, and over all of those rose petals, was Prince!

Every one of us cheered!

It was as beautiful a moment as you could possibly hope to see.

Then, as we watched Prince run across the bridge, out of the light walked a woman with a big, happy smile on her face. "Prince! Prince! Come here, Boy!! It's me, Mom!!!"

Prince ran faster than he ever had in *any* lifetime and leapt right up into his mother's welcoming arms! He kissed her face and she laughed and laughed. He jumped up and down and ran in circles all around her!

The most exciting thing of all was when we all heard Prince say, *"I love you, Mom!"* And she actually heard him! She heard his **own** voice, not as a bark, but as one she fully understood. Then we watched as they both walked away across a smaller rose-covered path into another magnificent white light to share some much needed time together.

I looked at Mandy and smiled. *"Wow! It doesn't get much better than that, does it?"*

She smiled back at me. *"Hen, people on earth always talk about 'happily ever after's, they even write books about them. But this...what you have just witnessed…is the greatest happily ever after of all.”*

Chapter Fourteen

The crowd of happy animals soon went along their merry old way, and just as I was about to head down to howl at a half a dozen full moons, Mandy said to me, *"Know what today is?"*

"Sure! It's Prince McMillan of Philadelphia Day!"

"Yes, that's true, but…"

"But?"

"Well, it's also a very special day for you too."

"Me? How come?"

"Henley…it's your three-month anniversary. You can use the monitors today!"

"I can?!!!"

"You sure can!"

In a flash almost as fast as my old pal, Prince, ran across The Rainbow Bridge, I ran toward the monitors. I scurried back and forth and back and forth waiting to see my name flash onto one of the screens. Then, finally, there it was – in HUGE sparkling letters – HENLEY HARRISON WEST.

"*Mandy? What do I do?!*"

"*You just touch the screen with your paw and ask for what you want to see.*"

"*But, if I ask to see Mom and then I ask to see Dad, can I go back and see Mom again?*"

"*Sure you can.*"

"*Mandy?*"

"*What, Hen?*"

"*Can they hear me? You know, Mom, Dad, the cats…*"

"*Well, I can't say no **or** yes for certain, but for the most part, in my experience, the answer is no.*"

"*What do you mean for the most part?*"

"*I mean, did you ever hear me talk to you when I was on the monitor and you were still on earth?*"

"*Ummm…you know, sometimes, I thought I heard you, but then I figured that it was just wishful thinking on my part.*"

"*Well, now you know it wasn't just wishful thinking.*"

I nodded my head. "*I understand.*"

Then I took a deep breath, brushed off both of my paws and touched the screen that sparkled with the name – HENLEY HARRISON WEST.

As my paw touched the monitor the screen turned blue and white and then those two colors swirled together.

I said, *"Hello, this is Henley and, umm…"*

"Go on," Mandy nudged, *"there's nothin' to it."*

"Monitor? I'd…I'd like to see my home, please."

Chapter Fifteen

All of a sudden the colors twirled faster and faster and then as things started to slow down other colors came into view. Then it slowed down even more and I saw that those colors were starting to take shape, and soon, there it was…that charming little green and white Cape Cod that I had called home for the last four years of my life.

"Look, Mandy! Home Sweet Home!"

She smiled at me.

"Looks like Mom's planting red geraniums in the flower boxes this year. They were always my favorite! Hey! Check it out!! In the back of the house! Dad's planted tomatoes, and cucumbers, and hot peppers!"

She nodded.

"And look! Birds in the birdbath! Aren't robins and blue-jays pretty?"

"You're asking a cat about birds?!"

"Oh, sorry. But, Mandy, look! There's the stone they placed there for you after you crossed The Rainbow Bridge. You know, I used to walk out there and say hello to you every day. I always said I love you and missed you and that you were my best friend."

"I know you did Henley. It always made me smile. See what else is there?"

"Another stone…"

"Yup. They put it there for you, so we'd always be together. Go on, read it."

The monitor zoomed in closer to the marker and I read it out loud:

If tears could build a stairway…
And memories a lane…
I'd walk right up to Heaven…
And bring you home again.

Mandy smiled. *"Hen…Once humans allow animals into their lives, they learn a lot more about life than they would have otherwise. They soften up and open themselves to the things that really matter. They think more 'outside' of their own lives. They're more giving and loving. There just nicer people in general. They really are."*

Immediately I felt the need to see my Mom and the computer took me to the large bedroom on the right side of the house. Mom was dusting the dresser and rearranging the picture frames. She looked just like I remember. I was so happy to see her I couldn't even speak.

I watched as she picked up the last photo and dusted it off. It was a picture from last Christmas when we were both getting ready to be a part of the annual Holiday Parade! Mom and I got to ride in my Uncle Bob's red Mustang convertible. It was really cool! The photo was taken on our front steps and I was wearing fuzzy red antlers and looked pretty darned cute if I do say so myself! Dad held the camera in his hand and Mom leaned in toward me and said what a sweet boy I was and then, just as I was about to give her a kiss on the face, Dad snapped the picture! I love that photo!

Mom looked at it for quite a while and then I heard her voice. I hadn't heard her speak for three months and it was music to my ears.

"Oh, Hen…what a great day we had, huh?"

We did, Mom.

"You were so wonderful. The kids all loved you. They LOVED the antlers! Remember that?!" she chuckled.

I remember.

Mom picked up the picture and gave it a kiss. "You'll always be my boy."

I will, Mom. I mean…I am! I'm still your boy!

I watched as Mom placed the photo back down on the dresser and then she headed toward the door. Mom opened it and called for my Dad, "Andrew? Did you just say something?"

"No, Sweetie-pie," he called back, "I'm workin' on the shelves for Henley's stuff! Why?"

"Oh, nothin'," she said as she headed down the stairs, I just thought I heard you say Henley was still my boy. Must've been something on the radio."

NO!!! THAT WAS ME!!!!! MOM!!!! YOU HEARD ME!!!!!

Chapter Sixteen

I asked the monitor to take me down to the basement and on my way there I saw Cassie and Abbey sleeping next to each other on the sofa. It looked pretty funny – these two huge sheepdogs, one on each end of the couch. They took up the whole thing!

Holly was chasing a toy mouse around the living room, Scaredy Cat Ned was hiding under the sofa, Miss Rose was having a drink of water and just as the monitor focused on Mookie, he seemed to look straight into the screen.

"Mookie?"

"Henley?!"

"HEY! Mandy told me probably no one could hear me, but Mom sorta did and you **really** *did!"*

"Well, hey, let's face it…I'm The Mookster, and The Mookster is not your average cat!"

I chuckled. "So, how are you, Mook?"

"I'm doin' fine, Hen. I've been visiting kids at lotsa schools with Mom. I love seeing the kids!"

I smiled. "I told you! I loved the children!"

"And rescue and adoption are important messages. I mean, if it weren't for rescue and adoption, you and I would have never had such nice lives. We were lucky, Henley. Now we need to make sure that every animal finds a happy forever home!"

"Lots of children and adults are trying hard to make that happen, Mookie."

"Well…Mom, Dad, Jonny, and I promise to do our part. You can count on that. Your mission goes on, my friend."

"Thanks, Mook."

"Hey…before I forget, you might want to say a few things to your Puppy Cat before you go."

"What's the matter?"

"She's still in a very uncat-like funk since you've been gone."

"Will do, Mookie."

"Say 'Hi' to Mandy for me, okay, Hen?"

"You can be sure of it."

"Oh hey…Henley?"

"Yeah?"

"How is it up there?"

"Heavenly, Mook…just absolutely heavenly."

Mookie smiled and then shook his head. *"I guess I shoulda figured that one out!"*

Then I asked the monitor to direct itself onto Cynthia, my Puppy Cat. She was sitting in my Henley bed with her head resting on the edge of it. She looked very sad.

"Cynthia?"

"Henley?!! Is that really you?"

"Hey! Remember I promised you that you'd hear from me again!"

"Oh, Henley, I just miss you sooooo much. I'm not even eating right these days."

"Cyn, listen to me. We're universal souls, animals of great pride and depth. The circle of life is what it is and what it will always be. Live a good and kind and loving life. Enjoy the time you have there. Live every moment filled with love and compassion and joy and strength. The Rainbow Bridge will be waiting in the wings. We'll see each other again."

"Oh, Henley...I'm so happy to hear your voice! I feel better already!"

"Good girl! Now go grab a bite to eat and get back to being the beautiful and loving cat that you really are."

"Will we talk again?"

"Cynthia, I promise you we will. Now go eat!"

"Okay, Hen!!!! I love you!!!! Thanks for visiting!!!!"

"I love you too, Puppy Cat!"

I immediately turned toward Mandy. "This is a totally amazing machine!"

She nodded. "Totally."

Chapter Seventeen

My next trek was to the basement to see Dad. I love Dad. There he was up to his neck in hammers and nails and wood and paint, creating beautiful shelves and a bookcase to put all of my stuff in. You know, all the wonderful letters that children would send to me after Mom and I visited schools and libraries, a few copies of the book I wrote, my stuffed toys, photos, and newspaper articles…lotsa cool things.

Dad! You are soooo wonderful!

I watched as my Dad turned around and smiled.

"Judy? Did you just say something?"

Mom walked down the steps and into the basement. "What?"

He gave her a BIG hug and a BIG kiss. "I heard what you said," he smiled again. "You said I was *sooo* wonderful!"

Mom smiled back at him. "It must've been something on the TV down here. I didn't say it, but I should have!" She returned his kiss, "Because you, my love, **are** *soooo* wonderful!"

NO!!! THAT WAS ME!!!!! DAD!!!! YOU HEARD ME!!!!!

Mandy chuckled. *"So much for reconnecting to our earthling 'uprights'."*

Chapter Eighteen

Next I asked to see where Jonny was and the monitor took me down the street in a whirl of color and straight into the convenience store where Jon always bought my treats.

There he was in line with a bottle of juice in one hand and two beef jerky sticks in the other.

"That'll be $4.17 please." The clerk smiled.

"I remember when it used to be $6.17."

"The price dropped that much?" the clerk asked.

Jon smiled back, "No, I just used to get two for me and two for our dog. He loved these things."

The young girl nodded.

"Great dog," Jon muttered as he walked away.

"He still thinks of me too," I said to Mandy.

"Hen, they all think of us. We were their family!"

"But Jonny seems kinda sad."

"Humans tend to linger on things…good things…bad things…sad things…. It's not just a done deal with them for the most part."

"But?"

"But what, Henley?"

"Well, why do they talk about The Rainbow Bridge as this wonderful place and yet they still ache over our loss? I know they need to cry, and feel sad…but they need to move on, too. To move on is to honor us in a very healthy way, right?"

Mandy nodded.

"They need to have more faith in what they believe in."

"Smart dog." She smiled at me.

Just then I watched as Jonny got into his car and headed back up the street – to my wonderful old Home Sweet Home.

I love ya, Jon Boy.

Chapter Nineteen

Mandy and I watched the traffic barrel along on Crescent Boulevard for a while, then the monitor flew us over the skyline of Philadelphia, right across the Betsy Ross Bridge. One happy memory after another came back to me and I wanted to see more and more of the earth that I had come to know and love.

One thing I did notice was that life is just so fast and complicated on earth. I never fully realized it when I was there. Mandy sat next to me as we visited people and places. It was fast, but it was fun.

My last two stops before visiting Mom and Dad at home again were two of the schools that I visited many, many times. In fact, I was the mascot at one of them!

Mom was a friend to animals all of her life and she would take me to schools with her to teach children about the importance of animal rescue and adoption. See, I was born in a puppy mill in Lancaster, Pennsylvania, and I was also the sickly runt of the litter, so I was abandoned there and left to die because puppy mills only care about selling the animals for a lot of money. And nobody can make money selling a sick puppy because no one wants one.

Luckily someone spotted me and called rescue, and as they say, the rest is history. Mom adopted me, and we had a wonderful life together. Mom also helped me write my life story and we toured schools with it to teach children that just because your life may start off in a bad place that doesn't mean you have to end up in that same bad place. 'Happily ever after's are out there! My message was also about caring for our animal friends, being a voice for those who cannot speak for themselves...and the children listened. And now as I look through my special monitor I can see that they still read my story and they continue to do right by our animal friends even without me there to help guide them.

I wagged my shaggy butt with joy!

Chapter Twenty

One quick request to my "HENLEY" monitor and I was back home again. Jonny was playing a game on his computer, and the juice and one beef jerky were already gone.

Mom and Dad were putting the final touches on the bookcase and shelving in the basement. And you know what? It looked pretty darn good to me.

Mandy and I watched as Mom placed a few of my toys inside one of the drawers Dad designed.

"I'll run upstairs and get a few more pictures of Hen for the wall. You know, ones with us and the cats and the dogs."

"Okay," Dad smiled. He sat down on the chair for just a moment taking in all of his handiwork. "I wonder what you'd have to say about all this, Hen."

Dad, I think you did a really great job.

He nodded to himself. "You know what, Hen? I bet you'd say. 'Dad, I think you did a really great job'."

Well how about that!

Chapter Twenty-one

One more paw tap on the monitor and I saw Mom up in the bedroom leafing through what seemed like at least a hundred pictures. And every photo Mom looked at she had a comment to make.

Mandy and I sat by the monitor and listened.

"Geez, Hen...look how young you were in this picture!...Look how cute you and Cynthia are in this one...Oh, here's you and Dad at the Rescue Picnic with Grannie Annie!...Here's me and you at school with all the kids..."

Then Mom came to the very last picture and so she gathered them all together and put them inside a large box and closed the lid on them.

I turned toward Mandy. *"I hope she doesn't get all sad and start to cry. Be strong, Mom. I'm here! I'm doin' just great! Honest I am! Believe, Mom! Believe!!!"*

Then I watched as my dear mother picked up the box and held it close to her chest.

"Hen…if you can hear me…"

I can hear you! Yes! I can hear you!!!!

"I just want to tell you how much I love you and to thank you for being such a joy in my life. …For teaching me the softer and gentler ways of living.

"Thank you for being such a good friend to your sheepdog sisters, to the children, to all the cats, our friends, family….

"You taught me strength and dignity. I learned that from watching you. You were more than my dog…you were my friend. See you again someday, Henley. I believe in The Rainbow Bridge…and I believe in you."

Then Mom carried the box out of the room and headed down to the basement – to my Dad.

I turned toward Mandy and smiled. *"Miss Manners, I think I'm done here for the day."*

"You are?"

"Yeah…I am."

"So, how did you like it?"

"Like it? Mandy, I loved it!"

Chapter Twenty-two

I put my paw on the monitor once again and said, *"That's all for today. Thank you so much!"*

The screen immediately went blank and another dog's sparkling name – CHARLIE 'DUKE' LAWSON, appeared to replace mine.

Mandy and I left the monitor area and then headed down toward Starland.

"So, what's on the agenda for tonight, Sheepdog?"

"Oh, I think I'll howl at a few full moons, go for a swim, stop by The Magical Tree and request some soft, fragrant, spring weather, and then just chill out with my very best friend."

"Which would be me, of course!"

"Of course!"

The two of us strolled just a bit further and then she turned to me and smiled.

"Hen?"

"What, Mandy?"

"Have you ever seen a cat howl at the moon?"

"Can't say that I have."

"Well then, my dear boy…" she chuckled, "YOU are in for a real treat tonight!"

The End ...?

Friends of Henley…

Best Friends Animal Society:
-A better world through kindness to animals-

Best Friends Animal Society is guided by a simple philosophy: kindness to animals builds a better world for all of us. In the late 1980s, when Best Friends was in its early days, roughly 17 million dogs and cats were being killed in shelters every year. Despite the commitment of shelter workers to the animal in their care, the conventional belief was that little could be done to lower that terrible number. Best Friends' No More Homeless Pets campaign created a new vision: A grassroots effort to place dogs and cats who were considered "unadoptable" into good homes, and to reduce the number of unwanted pets through effective spay and neuter programs. Since then, the number of dogs and cats being destroyed in shelters has fallen to approximately five million a year. There has been much progress, but there is still much more to do. The next phase of this work – bringing the number down to essentially zero – will take more work and some bold new initiatives. Shelters are crowded with pit bulls, dogs abandoned after being bought from pet stores, stray cats rounded up on the streets and not looking their very best when they're brought in, and other pets abandoned or neglected.

As the flagship of a grassroots network of people and organizations that care about animals, Best Friends continues to lead the way toward this future. And that's why our purpose remains: A better world through kindness to animals.

PLEASE contact them today!

www.bestfriends.org

ASPCA:

The ASPCA was founded in 1866 as the first humane organization in the Western Hemisphere.

The society was formed to alleviate the injustices animals faced then, and they continue to battle cruelty today. Whether it's saving a pet who has been accidently poisoned, fighting to pass humane laws, rescuing animals from abuse or sharing resources with shelters across the country, the ASPCA works toward the day in which no animal will live in pain or fear. Please join them in the fight to end animal cruelty! Become a member of the ASPCA today!

www.apsca.org

ASPCA 24-Hour Animal Poison Information!

If your pet has swallowed anything you fear is poisonous, please call the ASPCA's National Poison Control Center:

888-426-4435

This is a toll-free call!

The SPCA of Philadelphia:

350 East Erie Avenue
Philadelphia, Pennsylvania – 19134
215.426.6300

www.pspca.org

The PSPCA addresses the needs of thousands of homeless animals each year. They started out with a single center in Philadelphia and with the help of dedicated staff and generous donors, burgeoned into a statewide operation with seven very busy shelters.

Please visit or support this facility in any way that you can. Help them materialize their mission – helping not only animals in need but also inspiring people to be more humane.

Bring out the best in yourself!

Adopt a pet today!!!

Petfinder.com

The Petfinder.com Foundation helps support the thousands of animal organization members of Petfinder.com by raising funds for them.

Their objective?

To increase the number of animal adoptions for homeless pets.

Petfinder changes lives.

They affect not only the four-footed animals waiting to be adopted, but also the people who care for them. They supply equipment and funds so that thousands of homeless pets have healthier and happier lives and thousands of shelter and rescue folks can do their jobs better.
Please make a donation today and visit their wonderful web site often!

www.petfinder.com

Neoesr.org

New England Old English Sheepdog Rescue, Inc.'s mission is to establish, organize, and maintain a rescue program for abandoned, mistreated, or unwanted Old English sheepdogs, like **Henley** once was, regardless of whether such animals are purebred or registered with the American Kennel Club.

People frequently ask me what has made our program so successful. My answer is that we have the ability to remain fluid. We avoid rigid policies. By remaining flexible, we have the cooperation of our volunteers. Each dog and adoptive home is evaluated on an individual basis. While the work is supervised, each volunteer is given a lot of choice as to how he deals with the evaluation of a given dog or adoptive home.

Placing a Rescue dog requires a lot of work, but the reward is in knowing we have saved a life or at least afforded an unwanted pet the opportunity for the good life he deserves. Our new owners are aware of how they have helped out an innocent furry creature who has run into some bad luck along the way. It's a happy ending for the dogs as well as their 'Uprights.'

Annie Raker - Founder

http://neoesr.org

Pets911
(pets to adopt in your area!)

www.pets911.com

Shelter and rescue organizations in this country are brimming with unwanted, stray and homeless pets.
Please do your part to alleviate this problem. With everyone understanding the issue, doing their part to care or their pets like family members, and utilizing the important resources PETS911 can offer your community, we can and will solve this issue!

If you don't have Internet access, adoption and care information is available via the PETS911 toll-free, bi-lingual phone line.
Please call us!

1-888-PETS-911

Dear Friends,

Please remember:

Always report animal abuse of any kind.

You must be the voice for these dear, sweet animals who cannot speak for themselves.

Also…please adopt a furry friend from a shelter, and not a pet store! And, have all your 'companimals' spayed or neutered and make sure that your pet is up to date on all of his or her shots.

We want to stay healthy so we can be around to love you for a long, long, long time!

XOXO,

Your Shaggy "Rainbow" Friend,

Henley

He is your friend, your partner, your defender, your dog.

You are his life, his love, his leader.

He will be yours, faithful, and true, to the last beat of his heart.

You owe it to him to be worthy of such devotion.

Made in the USA
Las Vegas, NV
16 February 2022